Elevate Beyond

**A Real World Guide to Standing Out in Any
Job Market, Discovering Your Passion and
Becoming Your Own Person**

JAKE KELFER

Elevate Beyond

A Real World Guide to Standing Out in Any Job Market, Discovering Your Passion and Becoming Your Own Person

Jake Kelfer

Cover Design by Cheyenne Samsel

To

My Parents, for giving me unconditional love and support...

My Brother, for giving me confidence...

David Stroud, for giving me inspiration everyday and being #StroudStrong...

And to you, for giving me a chance.

Contents

Acknowledgments

I have so many people to thank for giving me the courage and support to write this book. First and foremost, I want to thank my parents, Dave and Sheri, for giving me the chance to pursue my dreams and follow my heart. Without your love and support, I never would have had the courage to write this book. It means the world to me that you didn't pressure me into getting a full time job right after college and because of that I've since had the opportunity to work for the Lakers, write this book, create a new online platform dedicated to inspiring and helping people achieve their definition of success, and work with dad on his newest business venture and help him live his dream. Nothing means more to me than family, so thank you!

Jonah, I didn't forget about you. Thank you so much for being the brother I've always wanted and needed. You've given me the strength to go against the grain and do things other people won't. I've learned so much from you and I only hope that when you make it big, we can do an awesome project together. I know I annoy you sometimes when I ask you to look at an article or give me your thoughts on a new idea, but you always do it and I truly appreciate it.

To my grandparents Nama, Poppy and Grandma: Thank you for always believing in me and telling me I can do anything I want to.

To Max Sommer: You are the only person that can get under my skin but keep me calm and collected. Thank you for your support and motivation.

To Lonnie Jackson: Thank you for opening my mind to the endless possibilities the world has to offer. You told me that we are here to help people and I hope that this book is able to help millions of people.

To the Kassan Family: Thank you for always being there for my family and me. Jake, thanks for taking me under your wing and always helping me out. Randi, thanks for your encouragement.

To Sergio Millas: Thank you for being a mentor to me. You've always inspired me to set big goals and never settle. You told me that the time to take risks is when you're young and if it weren't for a phone call we had, I might not have written this book. Even more so, you've engrained in my brain that every problem has a solution; I just have to find it.

To Mrs. Ferry: Thank you for being a huge supporter of mine since high school. You always gave me that extra boost of confidence that I could achieve anything I set my mind too.

To Devyn O'Brien: Thank you for letting me run your ear off at any moment of any day. It takes a special person to listen to me all the time and I appreciate it.

Thank you Brian Bloch, JB Kalin, Brock Vereen, Jake Kassan, Jeff Fellenzer, Uncle Stan, Ben Badower, Max Miller, Brandon Berman, Easton Fier, Blake Pinsker, Taylor Harrison, Rahul Bansal, Chase Lehner, Emily Dods, Chase LaVine, and Sasha Spivak for allowing me to share your stories.

Thank you to everyone who picks up this book so you can have a better life. I appreciate your willingness to grow and I am happy to be apart of your journey!

Introduction

I've always been one to elevate my life and go beyond what is expected. Ever since I can remember I've always wanted to level up all aspects of my life. I wanted to be the best basketball player, the best student and the best person I could be. Academically, I loved learning so much that I taught myself Algebra II/ Trig in 8th grade and I took Calculus my sophomore year of high school. Athletically, I loved playing sports and was blessed to be able to compete with players who were older and more skilled than me. I was also fortunate to play against athletes who are now in the NBA, NFL and MLB. Socially, I loved talking so much that I became friends with everyone I could and I became a family favorite. I always loved talking to my friends' parents and learning from them. Throughout my life, it didn't matter what I was doing; all that mattered was that I wanted to learn, become a better person, and positively influence those around me.

By the time I got to high school, I realized that everything I did would influence my future and I knew that graduating from USC and making my impact on the world were two things I wanted in my future. I realized at that time that everything I had done before and everything I would be doing from that point forward was to achieve those goals. I got involved in clubs, sports, community service, and I made sure my grades were the best they could be. By the time I finished high school, I was extremely proud of everything I had accomplished but until I received my acceptance letter from USC, I wasn't satisfied. Finally after what seemed like months of waiting, I received my acceptance letter and my dream of being a Trojan was a reality!

When I walked on the USC campus as a freshman, I knew I had found my new home. I saw the opportunities that were ahead of me and I couldn't wait to get started. Classes were important to me and I wanted to make sure I learned and earned good grades, but the thing that was most important and exciting to me was gaining access to the Trojan Network. I knew that if I wanted to change the world and make the biggest impact, I would have to meet everyone I could and build a relationship with them. I realized early on that college was not just about academics; it was also about having fun. It is a time to find out who you really are and prepare yourself for the rest of your life!

During my four years at USC, I did my best to make the most of my college experience. I wanted to do well academically, socially and athletically, but even more so I wanted to set myself up for my future. While I enjoyed going to fraternity parties, winning intramural championships, creating my own company and running different organizations, I knew that my college experience would set the stage for the years to come. Since I knew that, I made sure to take advantage of all of the guest speakers, seminars, mock interviews, and resume workshops I could find. I was constantly on LinkedIn or setting up informational interviews because I wanted to learn as much as possible from as many people as I could. I put in the work and learned the ins and outs, so that when the time came for me to get an internship or job, I would be prepared. All that hard work paid off, as I was able to secure internship after internship. Not only that, but by the end of my senior year, I was able to give dozens of students advice and help them reach their academic, networking, and career goals.

Now, one year after college, I have worked for the Los Angeles Lakers, started another business, spoke at my alma mater, and wrote a book. Everything I've done is part of my life mission: to enjoy my journey and to help inspire others on their journey to personal success and happiness. As I share this book with you, I hope that you will be helped in one way or another as you embrace and continue your life journey. If just one person expands his/her network or learns one success tip from this book, I will know I have made an impact on the world.

This isn't your ordinary book. It isn't 300 pages of information or full of new discoveries. This book is, however, a compilation of strategies, tips, suggestions, and experiences for students to utilize to improve their chances of standing out in any job market. There are actionable exercises, real call scripts from informational interviews, sample networking emails and much, much more. This book is a summation of everything I've learned from college professors, my own informational interviews, dinners with executives, business meetings, resume workshops, and networking events. I don't know everything about this topic, nor will I claim to, however, I do know hard work and what it takes to stand out and have a positive impact on my life and the lives of others around me. I know what it is like to be a college student and person who succeeds.

This book will not only contain many of the strategies that I learned and used to obtain the jobs I wanted, but also it will feature tips and advice from the best in the business including professors from USC, professionals from a financial services firm, Apple, MVMT Watches, and a professional athlete. It will give you a competitive advantage over everyone else and provide ways to maximize success without having to waste hours or spend hundreds of dollars for college counseling, private tutoring, resume seminars or networking workshops. By using these tips and implementing the strategies mentioned in this book, you will have the tools needed to get ahead of the competition and be one step closer to having the chance to succeed in the workforce and life.

Now, I don't want you to read this like a normal book. I want you to take a look at the different chapters/topics and read them in order of *what is most important for you to learn* and for you to achieve your definition of success. Also, throughout the book there will be exercises that will help you process the information. I am also happy to share Kelf Keys with you which are added bonuses for your benefit and entertainment.

This book is meant to teach, reteach, or otherwise hone your skill set to be the best candidate and person possible. I chose to make this book as simple and timeless as possible, so that it remains just as effective in the future as it does now. I've handpicked the greatest advice I've ever given and the greatest lessons I've ever been given.

IF AT ANY POINT WHILE YOU'RE READING THIS BOOK AND HAVE QUESTIONS, PLEASE DON'T HESITATE TO REACH OUT.

YOU CAN BEST CONTACT ME ON THE FOLLOWING SOCIAL MEDIA CHANNELS:

INSTAGRAM: @JAKEKELFER

TWITTER: @JAKEKELFER

SNAPCHAT: JKELF

FACEBOOK: facebook.com/jakekelferjourney

WEBSITE: www.jakekelfer.com

EVEN IF YOU DON'T HAVE ANY QUESTIONS, I'D LOVE FOR YOU TO STOP BY AND SAY HELLO. IF YOU WANT TO REACH ME IN PRIVATE YOU CAN EMAIL ME AT

JAKEKELFERJOURNEY@GMAIL.COM

Life Tips Essential To Any Career

Hustle

Hustle. Hustle. Hustle. In order to be the best or even just really good at your job and life, you have to hustle. There is no substitute for hard work. Jocks and nerds alike all have to hustle if they want to be successful. As you read this book, remember to keep hustling, keep working harder than everyone, and keep pushing through any obstacle that may be standing in your way. When you do that and combine the strategies and tips in this book, you'll become a fierce competitor in the game of life.

Provide Value That Makes You Irreplaceable

When you first start out you will have to find ways to add value to whatever company you work for. Be willing to do whatever you have to in order to make a difference. Do the things no one else wants to because that is how you get noticed. As an intern, whenever you are asked to do something, say yes and say yes with a smile on your face. No task is too small. The more you are willing to do things others won't and the better attitude you have the more valuable you become. You become a reliable employee that is hard to replace which increases your chances of getting hired.

Have a Desire to Learn

There's nothing more appealing to an employer than someone who has a desire to learn and grow in life. Life is full of lessons and if you have a desire to learn, you will be successful. Some of the most successful people in the world read everyday because they want to continue learning. I hope that this book will teach you some invaluable lessons, but even more so I hope that you will take it upon yourself to continue learning and growing even after you begin to climb the ranks.

Be Comfortable With the Uncomfortable

Part of life is trying new things and developing your true character. As you go through life and experience the workplace you are going to be placed in situations and asked to complete tasks that might not feel comfortable at first. As long as the situations and tasks fit with your values and ethics, do them. Learn to be comfortable and adaptable to the uncomfortable situations, thus you will be able to have a growth mindset and increase your success.

Have Fun!

You will hear this time and time again. Have fun on your journey! You are going to have ups and downs in your life but as long as you enjoy yourself, you will have more ups than downs. When you have fun, your quality of life will be better and you will find new opportunities in things you did not know existed. Life is too short to worry about the little things, so live in the moment and have a blast on your path to success.

Now let the journey begin!

Chapter 1: Discovering a Career You are Passionate About

"Choose a job you love, and you will never have to work a day in your life."

— Confucius

"Find out what you like doing best and get someone to pay you for doing it."

— Katharine Whitehorn

"The only way to do great work is to love what you do. If you haven't found it yet, keep looking. Don't settle."

— Steve Jobs

What are you going to do after high school? What are you going to do after college? Do you know what you want to do? Have you figured out your entire life yet? We've all been asked these questions at one point or another. The crazy thing is, most people have no idea how to answer them. Millions of people every year, every month, every day, and every minute are unsure of what they want to do as a profession and that is totally okay. Life is not meant to be figured out all at once. It is meant to be a process of continuous growth and learning experiences.

Some people know what they want to do from the minute they enter college or even high school for that matter. I tell them, good for you and good luck! But they are the rarity. The majority of people have no idea what they want to do or how to do it. For a lot people who don't know what they want to do, they end up taking a job just for the sake of having a job. Not just that, but a lot of people go through multiple jobs before they find one that is tolerable, let alone one they enjoy.

However, the more you try and the more you learn, eventually you will find a job that you are passionate about. Having a job is great especially during tough times, but imagine if you could have a career doing something you are truly passionate about. Making money and doing what you love. Isn't that the name of the game?

That's why this chapter is broken down into four actions and exercises that will help you figure out what job is the perfect fit. You will see that after each lesson, I've included how I went through this process to obtain my dream internship with Relativity Sports while I was in college. I hope that after reading this chapter and using the actions suggested, you will find a great start for your professional career.

The four questions you are going to ask yourself are:

- What interests me?
- What jobs are available within my interests?
- What do I need to know about these jobs?
- Did I find my calling?

Here we go!

Action 1: What Interests Me?

Think about what interests you and write a list. Interests can be anything: something that catches your attention, a hobby, something that you think is cool, a job that one of your friends has, or even something that might be fun to try. I want you to really dig deep and think about this. If you are going to have a job and career that you are passionate about, it starts with doing something you already like to do. If you like alcohol or dancing, don't be afraid to list them. Just because they might not seem like something you can turn into a job at first glance, it does not mean there are not opportunities within those interests. Once you write down your interests, separate them into categories so it is easier to see the variety of interests and where there is overlap.

Here is a quick list of my interests. You can see that sports and business are the two categories that really stand out to me. When this happens, it is great because there is often a way to combine the two when looking for a job.

Sports

- Basketball
- Baseball
- Football
- Olympics

Business

- Sales
- Marketing
- Negotiating
- Analytics
- Team Building
- Entrepreneurship

Hobbies

- Playing pickup basketball
- Social media
- Public speaking and inspiration
- Coaching
- Working with people with special needs
- Working with celebrities and athletes
- Blogging and reading

Action 2: What Jobs are Available?

Now that you have a huge list of interests, you need to find out what jobs are available within those interests. Go online to begin searching for the different jobs in those fields. For example, if an interest is sports, type "jobs in sports." A quick heads up, if you use a broad interest like sports there are going to be millions of options. I recommend narrowing down your search by combining it with another interest or separating it by location. If you want to be more specific, type in "jobs in sports marketing California." This will narrow down your search and help uncover options that are relevant to your goals.

As you continue to search and learn more about the different jobs within your interests, create a list of jobs and companies that catch your attention or intrigue you. It is important to understand that there are millions of jobs and every industry is different, so if you don't find the perfect job right away, keep looking.

In sports alone, one can work for a team, agency, league or even a company with a sports division. Within a team, one can work in sales, marketing, social media, graphic design, sponsorships, coaching, player development, and much more. I am not telling you this to overwhelm you, but rather to help you understand that there are so many opportunities out there; you just have to find the right one. Honestly, that's what makes this process fun and exciting. You might start with one interest and it leads you to a different one that actually becomes more interesting than the original interest you wrote down.

Once you complete your search, write down specific jobs or companies that interest you.

As I was heading into the summer after my junior year, I knew that I would have to find an internship or part time job. After doing a lot of the research based on my interests and meeting some great people, I realized that I wanted to work for a sports agency and learn the ins and outs of the agency world. I loved that sports agencies encompassed a lot of my interests from sports to business to negotiating to working with athletes. I found all the different ways to be an intern or part time employee as well as all the agencies that I found interesting. You can see below.

Jobs Available

- Marketing Intern
- Social Media Intern
- Digital Media Intern
- Football Intern
- Basketball Intern
- Baseball Intern

Companies

- Priority Sports
- Relativity Sports
- BDA Sports
- Creative Artists Agency
- Athletes First
- WME

Action 3: What Do I Need to Know?

Now that you have a list of jobs and companies that you are really interested in, it is time to learn what they are all about. To do this, you should do two things: connect and research.

Connect with people that work for the companies or jobs on your list. You can do this by emailing, calling, or connecting on LinkedIn. You will want to use your network to find people that you can get in touch with and learn directly from them. Refer to chapter 4 to see how you can build and utilize your network to help you learn more.

Also, research the companies and jobs to see reviews, salary ranges, job description, etc. You want to be as informed as possible and make sure that the job is in line with your career goals. If you want a job in sports, but are not willing to work extremely long hours, then it might not be the right industry for you. Doing the research now will help you eliminate some jobs that you think you like, but in actuality you just liked the idea of the job.

Keep in mind that when you are looking for an entry-level job or even a second job, you probably will not be able to secure a job as VP of Marketing. You will probably start as a Marketing Coordinator. Every company has their titles and job descriptions listed differently, so make sure to read through everything.

> **Kelf Key: Use Glassdoor to learn all about the jobs and companies you are interested in.**

As you research here are some questions you might want to have answered:

- What is the work schedule look like?
- Does the company work holidays?
- What kinds of benefits are there?
- How much does someone in this specific role make?
- Does it seem like there is room to grow within the company, both financially and in status?
- Will I get to work with higher ups?
- Will I have a mentor or be on a team?
- Is it commissioned or not?
- Does the job involve travelling and if so, how much?

All of these questions are very important, as they will help you get a better understanding of how the job aligns with your overall goals and passion. At this point of the process, you should know everything you want to know about the different jobs and companies that interested you in step two.

Before you move onto the next and final step, select a few jobs that are at the top of your list and use them for the final step.

As I went through this process of learning about the different companies and jobs, I came to the conclusion that I wanted to work in football or basketball at an elite agency. Each agency had their own perks such as a huge and well-known client list or great recommendations. Relativity combined my interests of entrepreneurship, marketing and sports. Priority Sports had a client list of great athletes and guys of great character that really interested me. Each agency had their pluses and minuses, so I set out to see which internship I could get.

Jobs That I Want to Pursue

- Football Intern at Relativity Sports
- Football Intern at Priority Sports
- Basketball Intern at Relativity Sports
- Basketball Intern at Priority Sports
- Basketball Intern at BDA Sports
- Basketball Intern at Creative Artists Agency

Action 4: I Think I Found a Match!

For the last and final step, take your top several jobs and look for openings and opportunities. Now that you have a great idea on what you want to do, it is important to fine-tune your resume and interviewing skills so you can be prepared for when you start the hiring process. I recommend asking your network for any leads and then begin looking at job sites and using LinkedIn. Also, you can go straight to the source as most companies will have openings listed on their website or on their LinkedIn page.

Kelf Key: Two of the most popular sites to use are Career Builder AND Monster. If you want to work in sports, I recommend Teamwork Online or Work In Sports. If you want to work in entertainment, I recommend Entertainment Careers.

Before I got my job with Relativity, I spent hours upon hours finding ways to get my foot in the door and my resume seen. I made sure that they were still hiring for the summer so I didn't spend unnecessary time trying to get a position that didn't exist. I used my network to try and find an introduction to the company. I worked on my resume to make sure it was polished and ready to go in the event

Relativity was ready for it. Everything I did during that semester was in preparation of getting that job. I knew it was what I wanted to do and there was an opening, so I gave it everything I had.

You've completed the four steps and hopefully have a better idea on the job you want and how to begin finding opportunities so celebrate your journey up to this point. The process of deciding on a career path let alone finding and obtaining a job you are passionate about is hard work. It is going to take time, but if you follow these guidelines, you should have a pretty good idea of what jobs are the best fit for you. That, to me, is worthy of a celebration.

> *Kelf Key: There is no one size fits all when it comes to finding a job. Everyone has a different path on his or her way to success, so have fun through the process.*

As I mentioned in the opening paragraph for this chapter, not only it is okay to not have the rest of your life planned out in your late teens or early twenties, most people do not. Life is a journey and we all have to start somewhere. After completing these exercises, you might find a job that you think you love only to find out it is not what you expected. You might have to go through two or three jobs before you find the perfect fit, but as long as you are willing to keep trying, you will find the right one. No matter where you are in your journey or career search, these principles will always be able to guide you on your next adventure.

Checklist

- Do you know your interests?
- Do you know what jobs are available?
- Do you know everything you can about the jobs you like?
- Do you have an idea of where to begin looking for jobs?

Worksheet

Put these exercises into action and find your passion. That alone will do for the first exercise.

Chapter 2: The Keys to Building an Irresistible Resume

"You will never get a second chance to make a first impression."

- Will Rogers

"If you can't make it good, at least make it look good."

- Bill Gates

How do I get my resume seen in a stack of 100 resumes? What should I include on my resume? How do I tell my life story in just one page? Building an irresistible resume is a process that evolves as you gain more life experience. At times you may get frustrated, but remember, with a great resume comes a elevated chance of getting a job. When you build a resume, it is important to be honest and true to yourself.

I bet you didn't know! From all of my interviews, recruiters spend anywhere from 30 seconds to 2 minutes on average reading a resume. Yeah, I know. It's not much time. That is why it is critical for you to follow these guidelines and use these strategies if you want to give yourself the best chance at your resume getting you to the next phase of the hiring process.

In this chapter, we are going to focus on three main characteristics that make for an irresistible resume.

- Appearance
- Content
- Personality

Each of these works together to make a winning resume that you will be proud of.

Section 1: Appearance

When creating an irresistible resume, one of the most important things is to make sure your resume looks good. We will get into the content and personality aspects soon, but the first impression is vital. Just like going on a first date, you want your resume to look its best. If you're like me, you'll shave, try on a few outfits to make sure you look sharp and then head out feeling like an absolute winner (or at least look like an absolute winner). This mentality should be the same when creating your resume. You should aim to create a resume that is aesthetically pleasing to the naked eye. When a recruiter first sees your resume, you want to leave them with no choice but to keep reading.

To make it very simple and easy for you to create a visually appealing, irresistible resume, I created a list of requirements that you must have to pass the appearance test. The best part about this test, everyone can pass!

The Appearance Test

Spelling and grammar *MUST* be correct

This might seem obvious, but you would be surprised at the amount of mistakes in this area. One of the easiest ways to get removed from the hiring process is to have spelling or grammatical errors. To ensure your resume has perfect spelling and grammar, use spell check, proofread, and ask a friend or family member to double check. It does not take much effort to do this right, so spend a few extra minutes to make sure your resume is mistake free.

Formatting *MUST* be easy to follow and understand

This means that everything needs to be formatted correctly. Everything needs to be easy to follow and understand. You will want to use the same font throughout your resume and utilize the **bold**, <u>underline</u> and *italic* features to help differentiate the segments on your resume in order to make your resume more visually appealing..

Consistency and Conciseness are a *MUST*

When you are putting together your resume, be concise and consistent. Tell your story in as few words as possible and make sure it flows nicely. Make sure that you are consistent with everything from your punctuation to spacing. When the recruiter looks at your resume, they want to be able to jump from section to section so if you are consistent and your formatting is correct, it will be easy for them to navigate through your resume and focus on the story you are trying to tell.

Submitting the PDF Version is a *MUST*

Whenever you send your resume electronically, make sure to always send it as a PDF. The reason for this is two-fold: this will preserve your desired formatting, (different versions of Microsoft Word might change the appearance); and, a PDF raises the barrier for someone else to change your resume. Once your resume is complete in Word (or another word processing program), save it as a PDF to your desktop. This way, it is easily accessible and much simpler to upload or send when you apply for jobs.

Kelf Key: Use resume paper when submitting your resume in person. For those of you that don't know what resume paper is, it is paper that is slightly different in texture and color than regular printer paper. It costs about $10 for 100 pieces and can be found at any store that sells office supplies. Think about it this way. If there are 500 resumes collected and 15 of them are a different color, the recruiter is more likely to look at the 15 that stand out because it catches his/her eye.

Section 2: Content

Now that you have passed the appearance test and your resume looks great, the next step to creating an irresistible resume is having content that tells your story in an organized, honest fashion. The first rule of thumb is to use reverse chronological order and list experiences from newest to oldest. Why? Because recruiters want to see your most recent accomplishments and experiences, not what you did five years ago. The content is your chance to humbly brag about your experiences and show recruiters the value you have added to companies, organizations, etc. The content portion of your resume, when done correctly, gives you the best chance to get to the interview stage.

When writing the content and describing your experiences that highlight and showcase your qualifications, make sure to include as much detail and specificity regarding what you did as possible. Also, when you can, include quantitative results so recruiters can easily see the great work you did. Saying that you increased revenue by 15% in 3 months sounds a lot better than saying you helped increase revenue and recruiters will take note of that. In a page filled with words, numbers stand out and that is the whole point!

Having great content is a huge component of being selected to the interview process because it shows your qualifications and experiences. To complete this section, here are some examples of great content that explain both the action and the impact. Feel free to use these as templates for your resume.

- Helped manage NBA Summer League social media accounts and increased Twitter presence by 25% up to over 50,000 followers

- Supervised proper execution of the $1M annual budget, creating a $50K surplus by the end of the year
- Organized a Habitat for Humanity volunteer day for 200 people, re-building 3 homes in 1 weekend
- Received the 2015 Salesman of the Year award by overachieving revenue targets by 50%
- Improved time management and teamwork skills by working 30 hours/week for a 10-week period while taking five academic classes

Section 3: Personality

The final piece to creating an irresistible resume is to add personality and a flair that will make your resume unique. Every person in the world is different and has something exceptional to offer, so why not show it?

This is your chance to impress recruiters before they make their decision on whether or not to put you through to the next round of the hiring process. If the recruiter does not remember you giving him or her your resume at a job fair or networking event or if you submitted it online, your resume is all the recruiter can base your personality off of.

Many people have different opinions about including skills and interests, objectives, or high school experiences but at the end of the day, add whatever makes you stand out. I would not suggest using high school experiences when you are in your junior year in college, but feel free to use them when you are just starting to gain experience. When you include some flavor on your resume, recruiters take notice.

The great thing about adding personality is that you never know what part of your resume is going to resonate with a recruiter and create a spark that will lead to a conversation. Here are some topics you can include that will help you stand out and lead the recruiter to asking for more.

- World traveller
- Bi or Multilingual
- Pets
- Community service
- Musical talent
- Love for reading

Section 4: Resume Advice from a Young Professional

During an interview I had with Brian Bloch, Financial Analyst at Apple iTunes, I asked him about his experiences on his path to securing a job at Apple. If there's one thing I've learned from him it is that there is no substitute when it comes to creating a great resume. The amount of work you put into your resume will reflect the job you get. He was kind enough to share his answers and also provide a list of five easily avoidable mistakes that I have added for your benefit. All of his answers are his own opinions and do not reflect the opinions of his employer.

7 of the Most Frequently Asked Resume Questions

What do you look for in a resume?
- Content and attention to detail

What is the first thing your eyes gravitate to?
- Depends on the formatting. See below.

How important is my GPA?
- Depends on what it is. Generally speaking, if you are coming out of school, recruiters will want to know your GPA. That said, if you have enough

good work/extracurricular experience, you might be okay leaving your GPA out.

How do I create a great resume if I don't have a lot of experience?
- Dig deep and think about what you can include. Have you done any volunteer work? If you are having trouble in this area, it may be an indication that you should get involved in some more extracurricular/volunteer activities.

How long on average do you spend looking at a resume?
- It depends on the size of the stack and what stage of the application process. At first glance, no more than a few minutes.

What is the biggest no-no?
- Bad formatting. If your resume isn't visually appealing, recruiters probably won't take the time to read it.

Is there anything that you love to see on a resume?
- I like to see some interests/hobbies that are not work related. It helps to bring you off the page as a person and not just a potential employee.

5 Common Mistakes You Can Easily Avoid

Too vague/ redundant

- Look at the bullet points and ask yourself: does this really say what I did, or is it just filling up space?
- Make sure each bullet says something new, not just the same thing said differently.

Too specific

- Look at the bullet points and ask yourself: would someone that hasn't done this job understand what I'm talking about?
- Try to avoid acronyms and jargon that someone reading the resume might not understand.

Too old

- Don't hesitate to take old jobs or clubs off your resume. What is old to you depends on how much else to put in its place. Just remember, more isn't necessarily better.

Too long

- A resume should be at most 2 pages (front and back of a sheet of paper), **ideally just one page**.

Lying

- The worst thing you can do is lie on your resume. The integrity of your resume is the beginning of a good relationship between you and your potential employer.

If there is one takeaway that I want you to focus on it is to be yourself and be authentic. You are an awesome, incredible person and your resume is your way of showing that. When you follow the guidelines and advice from Brian Bloch along with the other sections of this chapter, you will be able to tell your story in an appealing and fascinating way that will translate into getting more callbacks, interviews and hopefully job offers.

Checklist

- Does my resume pass the appearance test?
- Is my content specific, detailed, quantitative (when applicable) and exciting?
- Does my resume show my personality and leave the recruiter wanting more?
- Am I being honest and staying true to myself?

Worksheet

Use the Facebook community to get a downloadable resume template. Request to join the **Elevate Beyond Book Community** group. All you have to do is download the template, input your information and add your own unique flair to it.

Chapter 3: Crushing the Interview

"It's just better to be yourself than to try to be some version of what you think the other person wants."

- Matt Damon

"Failing to prepare is preparing to fail."

- John Wooden

"Always be yourself, express yourself, have faith in yourself, do not go out and look for a successful personality and duplicate it."

- Bruce Lee

In all parts of life, you are always being interviewed. You are interviewed every time you meet someone new. People formulate opinions of you and try to get a feel for who you are the first time they meet you. Right or wrong, people will judge you based on the way you look, the way you talk, the way you carry yourself, and the way you make them feel. As we talk about interviewing strategies in this chapter, it is essential to understand that interviews happen all of the time and in all aspects of life.

Interviews can come in many different situations. They can be interviews for jobs where you meet with companies to find out if you are right for the job. They can be in sports where you have to show your leadership and character to see if teams want you to play for them. They can be on dates where you find out if you and your date are compatible with one another. They can be in the form of an introduction between an entrepreneur and a potential investor or customer.

They can also be in the form of a chance meeting with a stranger at a coffee shop. Regardless of what you are interviewing for, finding a way to stand out will help you accomplish your goals. This chapter will provide you with strategies and advice that can separate you from the rest of the candidates and make you the company's number one choice.

I, along with the people I've worked with and learned from, have all used these tips and strategies to create a memorable interview and ultimately, land a job. Let me tell you a secret, they work. I've added a list of common interview questions in the worksheet for this chapter for you to learn from and help you prepare for all of life's interviews.

Section 1: 8 Tips to Crush Every Interview

Interviewing for the job is the final step before you get hired. It is your chance to meet with your future coworkers and bosses to see if you are a fit for the company and to see if the company is really a fit for you. Your interview is the time for you to showcase your personality and qualifications, which up to this point in the process have only been seen online or on paper via your resume. It is the time for you to show why you deserve the position and what you will bring to the company, organization, partnership, etc. if hired.

Often, the interview stage is the most nerve-wracking part of the hiring process because people put a lot of pressure on themselves to do well. Some people go into an interview with the thought that if they don't get this job, they are a failure. Other people get nervous when they have to speak about themselves in front of interviewers. Whatever the case may be, it is important to realize that everything happens for a reason and if you don't get this job, you can always get another one. When you have this mindset and use the strategies mentioned in this chapter, you will be able to crush every interview and elevate your chances of being hired. Plus, you might even save yourself a few gray hairs in the process.

Dress to Impress

When you go into an interview you should always wear a suit unless otherwise specified. If you are not sure whether or not you should wear a suit, ask the recruiter before showing up. Some jobs will have different dress code requirements, so it is totally acceptable to ask the recruiter before going to the interview for the dress code. It's better to be safe than sorry. It is rare to lose an opportunity for being overdressed. Being underdressed, on the other hand, can cause for immediate removal from the hiring process.

> *Kelf Key: If your interview is early in the morning, plan out your outfit the night before, so the only thing on your mind is crushing the interview.*

Do Your Research

Before showing up for your interview make sure that you have done your research. You should research the company, the industry, and the interviewer/s.

By researching the company, you will enter the interview armed with knowledge and information that can help you respond to their questions, describing your responses with more details and presenting yourself as well educated. You will be able to discuss the company history or current projects the company is working on. For example, when I interviewed with the Lakers, I made sure to know as much as I could about the history of the team, the current roster, who their brand partners were, and what they have done in the past, so if I was asked about it, the interviewers could tell I was knowledgeable and did my homework.

Researching the industry is important because it will show assertiveness and willingness to go above and beyond. Think about this... If you are in the interview and the interviewer asks you for your opinion regarding the newest trend, you'll be able to provide a sophisticated answer because you are prepared. An interviewer will be impressed that you know so much, thus earning you bonus points. Interviewers want to see that you are invested in the industry the job is in because they want to know that you are going to be committed to the job and the company. If you know about the industry, you will be able to use your knowledge to seek out new opportunities and provide extra value once you have the role.

Lastly, make sure you research the people interviewing you as they are typically the main decision maker or at least on the team of decision makers. You should do this because you want to appeal to their personality and make the interview more of a conversation between two people than a Q & A. If you know someone's interests or tendencies, you can use that to your advantage with the content of your responses, tone of your voice, or questions at the end. The key here is to be able to develop some sort of emotional connection with the interviewer because when you do this, he/she is going to remember you more. To research the interviewer, the best ways are to look at their LinkedIn profile to see past jobs and interests and to search the company website to see if you can find more about his/her job responsibilities.

Prepare Questions

At the end of every interview, the interviewer will ask, "Do you have any questions for me?" I can't stress enough the importance of having questions prepared for this part of the interview. Just as they are interviewing you, you need to have questions to interview them. You have to make sure that the company culture and your potential coworkers are people that you want to work with. You have to make sure that this is the right fit for you because it would be a shame if you went through the entire process and spent hours of your time preparing and researching only to find out that you don't really like the role or the people that work there. When it comes to your turn to interview them and ask your questions, you should have a prepared list because you want to show the interviewer that you are genuinely interested in the role and learning more about the company.

The questions can be company specific or custom created for the interviewer. They can be anything that you want to know about the work place. They can also be formulated during the interview about something that you want to know and learn more about.

Here is a list of questions that I've accumulated and asked over the years for your benefit:

- What is your favorite part of the job and what would you like to improve?
- How would you describe the company culture?
- What has been your journey that led you to this point?
- What are some of the day-to-day responsibilities of the role?
- Will I have the opportunity to meet the rest of the team and the people I will be working with?
- What skills make for a great candidate?
- Who will I be working with on a daily basis?
- What is something that you would like to see completed in my first few months?

- What is the career path for someone in this type of role?
- What is the salary range?
- Are there benefits?
- Is there anything else you would like to hear about my background?
- When can I expect a decision?
- What is the next step in the process?

Arrive Early

"If you're early, you're on time. If you're on time, you're late."

– Unknown

Make sure that you arrive early on the day of your interview. Being late is a huge turnoff and can drastically decrease your chances of being hired. You should always get to the interview early and if you are more than 15 minutes early, you should sit in your car and visualize how great you are going to do. If you took the bus or train, find a coffee shop down the street and prepare there. With about 15 minutes before your interview, it is acceptable to check in and wait in the lobby.

If you are unfamiliar with the area or the company is located in the heart of a big city, drive to the location a few days before at the time of your interview. See how long it takes, whether there is traffic, and what the parking situation is like. Doing this ensures you will arrive on time on the day of the actual interview. It will also reduce some stress, as you will not have to worry about making it on time, thus you can spend your energy focusing on how calm, cool, and collected you will be during your interview. And, if you are nervous, don't forget to take deep breaths.

Listen First, Speak Second

When you are being interviewed, you should always listen. I don't mean just hear what they interviewer is saying. I mean listen; keep your ears open and be attentive. Respond with subtle nods to show you are hearing everything the interviewer is saying. Not only will this make you seem more interested, but it will allow you to gain a full understanding of what the job really is. It will help the interviewer feel that you truly care and you will be in a position to be able to engage and communicate better because you will be fully invested in the interview and not distracted by thinking about what may happen next.

Be Polite to Everyone

You never know who you might meet or talk to so be respectful and polite to everyone. Some companies will actually place executives and decision makers in weird situations to test your character and see how you interact with people. For example, sometimes companies will place higher ups in the receptionist area/ desk, so they can see your first interaction upon entering the work place. Be polite to everyone and you will be sure to impress and befriend everyone in the workplace. Oh, and being polite is just the right way to live!

Someone told me a story in college that changed the way I thought about life. It was the day of her final interview for her dream company and she got to her interview 15 minutes early and checked in. The receptionist told her that they were running late and to hang out in the lobby and make herself feel at home. Instead of sitting and playing on her phone, she used this opportunity to get to know the receptionist and find out more about her experiences with the company. She said hi to the custodians, the other employees and everyone else that she came across because she wanted to make a great first impression on the people she might soon work with. When it was finally time for her interview, she politely dismissed herself from her conversation with the receptionist and went into her interview. The interview ended up lasting only 20 minutes. For those of you that do not have a lot of interviewing experience, that is very short for a final round. When she finished up her interview, she thought she did well but she was not sure because of how short the interview was. Either way, she walked out, said goodbye to the receptionist and told herself that she did the best she possibly could have and whatever happens she will have to be okay with it. The next day she received a call from an unknown number. She assumed it was the company calling her back, so she answered the call. It was the company, but more specifically it was the receptionist. The receptionist reintroduced herself and said that she was not the receptionist; she was actually the hiring manager for the company. The actual interview took place in the waiting room and because she was so polite to the receptionist and everyone that walked by, she got the job. This is why is it so important to treat everyone with respect and see everything as an opportunity even if it does not seem like one at first.

Be Yourself

When you interview it is imperative that you be yourself and show your personality. This is the time to bring your resume to life and show them how great and deserving of the job you are. Interviewers want to see the person behind the resume. They want to see your authenticity and who you really are. The biggest piece of advice I've learned is don't try to be the person you think they want to hire because if you do, you will never know if the company is the right fit. Too many times, people try to present themselves as someone they are not and instead of that helping them, it actually hurts them. Be yourself and when you get the job, it will be because of who you are, not because of who you tried to be.

Have Fun!

Smile. Smile. Smile. Every interview is a chance to take the next step in your future, so have fun and enjoy the opportunity. When you have fun and smile, your positive energy will take over and interviewers will love your attitude. I know it is tough, but don't add extra pressure to yourself by thinking this interview is your only chance to get a job. Instead, look at the interview as the next part of your journey. If it is meant to be and you prepare properly, you will do great. If you get nervous or worried, just know that I, along with all of your friends, support you!

Section 2: What Do Interviewers Look For?

Similar to the resume section, I interviewed a professional who has had some early success with the interviewing process, both as an interviewer and interviewee. JB Kalin is a Private Wealth Management Analyst for a financial services firm. He is funny, compassionate, energetic, and a Taco Bell lover- not quite your typical finance employee.

> *Kelf Key: The next time you go to Taco Bell, order the Cheesy Gordita Crunch. You won't be disappointed. Or if you're like JB order the Crunchwrap Supreme.*

Outside of work, JB can be found volunteering at the Los Angeles LGBT Center or coaching Goalball for the Junior Blind of America. JB shared some of his first thoughts and tips to remember regarding the interview process. I provide these answers in hope that you will see that you can still be yourself and get the job you want.

How early should I arrive?
- Be in office at least 10 minutes before scheduled interview.

What should I wear?
- Suit (men or women). Better to be overdressed than underdressed. Shows that you care.

What should I bring?
- Resume, pen and paper to take notes. Business cards if you have them. You don't need anything fancy.

What types of questions will I be asked?
- Most important is "why do you want this job and what are you looking for in this role?" This is a great test of how much you really want the job and whether you truly understand the position.

Is there anything I can do to prepare?
- Don't script your answers, and don't try to memorize anything about yourself or the job. Practice rationalizing your thoughts so that you are comfortable creating concise statements that flow naturally.

How long should my responses be?
- As long as you feel is necessary without being redundant. If you feel that you are repeating yourself, wrap it up. Don't try to fill the silence after your response with unnecessary comments.

What are some characteristics you look for in a candidate during an interview?

- Confidence but not overconfidence - you do not want to appear arrogant. Eye contact is key (everyone knows this but often forgets once the interview starts). Smile... it gives a great impression and it will tell your brain to enjoy the process, which should also help keep you relaxed.

How can I separate myself from the other candidates in the interview room?

- Enthusiasm! Do your best to give the impression that you want this job more than everyone else.

How many questions should I ask at the end of the interview?

- One or two well-thought-out questions are better than rattling off a handful that you memorized. It is even better if you ask a question that follows up on something discussed earlier in the interview. Listen to the interviewer's answer. It may trigger a couple more questions which turns into a conversation, which is what an interview should really be.

What should I do after the interview?

- Write an email or hand-written thank you note to each of your interviewers. Do your best to make it as personal as possible.

Section 3: What Makes You Stand Out?

So far in this chapter, you've learned some of the best interview tips and what a young professional from the finance industry looks for. Now you are going to see how one NFL player improved his draft stock by being a great person and interviewer. It is important to note that no matter what field you want to be apart of you will need to interview. Whether it is finance, sports business, entrepreneurship, or the NFL you will need to interview and demonstrate why you deserve the job. No one understands this better than New England Patriots Safety, Brock Vereen.

Brock Vereen is an NFL player who was drafted by the Chicago Bears in the 4th round of the 2014 NFL Draft. He went to college at the University of Minnesota and completed his degree in Communication Studies. Brock is the younger brother of New York Giants Running Back, Shane Vereen, and the son of Henry and Venita Vereen. Brock shares his experience of the pre-draft interview process:

> "The NFL combine is one of the most pivotal steps in the draft process. Coaches, owners, trainers, and many other representatives from each of the 32 teams gather in Indianapolis to analyze prospective

rookies to see which players would make the best fit in their organization.

The difficulty in performing in a pre-draft interview is the fact that no two are the same. Some teams interview you with their entire staff in attendance while others just the coaches. Although it would seem these interviews would be pretty straightforward, it is very rare that football is the only topic of discussion. Through my experience there were multiple times where the topic of football never even came up. What you come to realize is that these teams are not just trying to find a football player. Like any other business, they are also looking for an employee. They are looking for someone who will represent their organization and be worthy of the salary that they are given. Your character is put on full display and often analyzed to a point of discomfort. The goal is to put you under as much pressure as possible and expecting you to give genuine answers.

When my pre-draft experience was over, my agent gave me a call to let me know that multiple teams had reached out to him to tell him that they thought I did a fantastic job and had carried myself like a professional. My success during this whole process was greatly due to knowing how to carry myself, how to keep my composure, and how to look the part.

Whether it is for the NFL or for a Fortune 500 company, being genuine is one of the most important factors in an interview. The players who enter the meeting room and try to be something they're not get written off immediately. These teams are looking to potentially invest millions of dollars in you; to think that they have not spent the time doing their research on you would simply be ignorant. It was somewhat easy to see during certain questions I was asked, that they already had the answer. The point of asking me the question was simply to see if I would look them in the eye and give them the truth, no matter how difficult it would be. The mental reminder to be myself before going into any office to meet with a team became part of my routine. On the flip side of things, one of the easiest ways to impress these coaches was to subtly show them that I had done some research on my end as well. These coaches and staffs are interested in you or else they would not be spending their time bringing you in. So for me to show that I knew what teams these coaches had coached for previously, where some of the staff members went to college, or if they had siblings also working in the NFL definitely went a long way to help the interview process. The best way to peak the interest of someone curious about you is to show him or her that the interest is mutual.

The phrase "be a professional" sometimes gets written off as cliché and gets washed out due to being overused. But the truth is in these cases it is the difference between millions of dollars. Every single year story after story circulates about a prospect who was unable to communicate and present himself in a respectful manner. The use of slang, slouching in a chair, not making eye contact, checking text messages, wearing gold chains to the interview are all things that sound ridiculous and common sense taboo, and yet seem to be instances that keep reappearing every year. These are the fastest ways to write yourself off of a prospective job with any team. A suit and tie was a must while visiting any team's facility during the pre-draft process. For example, on my interview with the Steelers, I vividly remember being pulled to the side by a coach who complimented me on my decision to wear a suit and tie. Showing how seriously you are taking the opportunity to meet with these teams is just another way of showing that mutual interest that can go such a long way.

It would be ridiculous to try to claim that personality and preparedness can trump the ability to play the game. A player who cannot perform on the football field, no matter how well he carries himself, will have trouble landing on a team. My point here is that not unlike any interview in corporate America, the interview stage during the pre-draft process should be seen as an opportunity to put your character on display to propel you ahead in the ranks of your peers."

Brock's character and respect for the interview process is a lesson that everyone can take away. Not everyone will have a chance to raise their draft stock, but everyone has a chance to raise their life stock and that is the key takeaway from Brock's story. Be yourself, be proud of what you are trying to accomplish, and be professional in every interview you have.

Section 4: Interviewing for a Non Traditional Job

If you are an entrepreneur, musician, actor, or someone who doesn't want a traditional 9-5 job, do not think for a second you will not have to interview. You might not go through a traditional interview process like you would if you were applying for a job at Google, Nestle, or Visa.

Instead, everyone you meet will be an interview. Everyone will want to find out as much about you and your business as they can. They will give you their thoughts and criticisms whether you ask for it or not.

As an entrepreneur, musician, actor or artist you will constantly be watched. You will be critiqued, complimented, hated, loved, etc. Regardless of what other people think about you or what you are doing, it is important to develop your interview skills because every time you give a pitch for investments, share new music, audition for a role or sell to a potential customer, you are being interviewed. Very rarely is an investor going to invest in an entrepreneur who is boring or who shows up late. Investors want to see the entrepreneur full of energy and passion and that he/she has a good business of course. A customer is going to be more likely to support an entrepreneur, musician or actor who dresses well and promotes his or her product with facts and sincerity. At the end of the day there is a direct correlation between how an individual presents him/herself and the success of the business.

Jake Kassan, the CEO of MVMT Watches was gracious enough to take some time and share his experiences and attitude towards interviewing. Jake is a college dropout turned successful entrepreneur. While school was not necessarily his thing, he always had a passion for starting businesses. People have called him a failure. People have called him a genius. Regardless of what people say, Jake has always carried himself with confidence and stayed true to himself. Turn your watches back and set some time aside to read his attitude toward interviewing and networking.

"I believe that as an entrepreneur you should always act as if you're being interviewed. To be honest I've only had one formal interview in my life, so I don't know much about them aside from the ones I have given in the last few years. My outlook is to treat everyone with respect and try to befriend as many people as I come in contact with. Back when I was a fresh dropout, I was working valet and opening car doors for millionaires and billionaires. You'd never think that the guy opening these doors would become the CEO of a multimillion-dollar business only three years later. I like to think the next person I'm kind too, befriend or share my past with will be that next success story you hear on TV. I do it for the people who did it for me but mainly for all of those people who didn't. A lot of successful people get lost along the way and forget where they started, but I like to think I leave a positive lasting impression and that people won't be able to find anything bad to say even if they tried.

This mindset is singlehandedly the most important reason why I am successful to this day. Being sincere, friendly, outgoing, and approachable with as many people will open up a huge network. This network will evolve rapidly, one person after another. With a world that moves so fast and technology that moves even faster, the one thing no one can steal away from you is your network. The most important and impactful events that have taken place in my journey have been simply by introducing myself or going out of my way to do something differently than the typical person. I am not a straight A Duke graduate. I do not know how to code and I am not a great salesman. I definitely did not reinvent the wheel. I am a college dropout who started a watch company in an overly saturated market and has become successful because of this mindset."

Jake's attitude and sincerity not only makes him a great individual but it sets the stage for those around him to be successful. He is always acting as if every introduction is an interview because he wants to be true to himself while also building relationships. This goes to show you that the approach Jake takes to being interviewed not only helps him be a likable person, but it also helps him develop his network and build genuine relationships which we will talk about next.

Checklist

- Do I know my story better than everyone else?
- Did I do my research?
- Do I have a list of prepared questions?
- Am I treating every introduction as an interview?

Worksheet

Answer these 15 frequently asked interview questions.

- Tell me about yourself.
- Why do you want this job?
- Why did you leave your last job?
- Why should we hire you?
- Tell me about a time when you had to overcome a challenge.
- Tell me about a time when you did not agree with a coworker. What did you do?
- What is most important to you in a new job?
- What are your weaknesses?

- What are three words that your friends would use to describe you?
- Where do you see yourself in five years?
- What are your goals?
- Random questions
  - If you were an animal, what would you be?
  - What is your favorite song and why?
  - How many tennis balls can you fit into a car?
  - How many potholes are in New York?

Do a practice interview with... yourself.

Go in front of the mirror dressed for an interview and bring a list of 5 interview questions. Ask yourself the questions out loud and then practice giving your answers. Hearing your own voice and seeing the hand gestures and body movements in the mirror will help you prepare for the real interview. It will be awkward at first, but it is a great way to build confidence and practice answering common interview questions.

Practice your story.

The first question everyone asks is "Can you tell me about yourself?" You want to answer this question in one minute or less. Be concise and focus on telling a story that is engaging and informative and fits with the job, subject matter, etc.

Visualize success.

For this exercise you are not going to physically do anything. You are just going to imagine yourself *crushing* the interview and getting your dream job.

- I want you to start by visualizing yourself getting dressed.
    - What color is your suit?
    - How is your hair looking?
    - Are you mentally prepared?
    - Are you feeling nervous? Confident? Excited?

- Next visualize commuting to your interview.
    - What music are you listening to?
    - Are the windows up or down?
    - What are you thinking about?

- You've arrived at the interview and have to wait a few minutes.
    - Are you making small talk with the receptionist?
    - Are you being polite to everyone who walks by?
    - Is your phone off?

- The time finally comes for your interview.
    - Are you respectful of the interviewers time?
    - Do you answer their questions with detail and confidence?
    - Do you ask questions?
    - Are you having fun?

- The interview is over and you nailed it.
    - How are you feeling?
    - Do you want to shout out loud when you get in your car?
    - Do you feel like you gave it your best shot?

- You arrive back at your home.
    - Did you send a follow up?
    - Are you happy that it is over?
    - Are you going to celebrate?

- You get the job!
    - What is going through your head?
    - Who is the first person you call?

- You did not get the job (Yes, this is still about visualizing success).
    - What did you do well?
    - What did you learn from the process?
    - What do you need to work on?

Chapter 4: The Path to Becoming a Champion Networker

"It's all about relationships, not just who you know, but who knows you!"

- Jeff Fellenzer

"Your network is your net worth."

- Guy Kawasaki

"I've learned that people will forget what you said, people will forget what you did, but people will never forget how you made them feel."

- Maya Angelou

Do you want to have a huge network? Do you want to have people in your life that will help you whenever you need it? Do you want a mentor that will guide you on your journey? Do you want to be someone who can help others? If you answered yes to any of these questions, then you are going to gain a lot of value from this chapter.

Building a strong network is one of the most important keys to success. Networking can be personal and professional but no matter which way you look at it, having a strong network is vital to success and growth in life. Having a network of people that you can trust and rely on helps you find new opportunities, professionally and personally, and will help you increase your future success more than you could ever imagine. Networking is all about building meaningful relationships and using those relationships to help improve the success, happiness, and lives of others in your network and around the world. One of the best parts about networking today is that you can meet and build relationships with incredible people from all over the world. You never know who you might be introduced to or meet, so keep an open mind and use every introduction as a networking opportunity.

We have all seen someone that we know we should talk to, but are scared to make the first move or fear how the person might react. I really want you to understand as we go through this chapter that everyone no matter what their title is, is still a person just like you and me. They have the same needs and feelings that everyone else does, so take a deep breath and make an effort to meet new people no matter who they are and grow your network.

Often times in school you are told to build a network and make connections. However, most people are left wondering what networking exactly is and how to do it. The most common questions I hear are, "I know I need to network, but how do I do it? Where do I begin? Should I just reach out to everyone I know and see if they can help?" For this chapter, you are going to learn a step by step networking process that will take you from thinking about the word networking to having the confidence to ask your network for job advice and recommendations.

Section 1: 6 Steps to Becoming a Champion Networker

Step 1: Commit to Networking

The first step to becoming a champion networker is to commit to meeting, talking and connecting with people. To be a champion networker, you really have to commit and be dedicated to the process. Making this commitment means that you are ready to accept the challenges and the rewards of building a strong network. It means you are willing to reach out to people that you may or may not know in order to make connections. You might face some rejection, but for every rejection, there is someone waiting to be contacted who will accept your invitation to connect.

It is important to note that networking is a long process that never ends unless you stop meeting people. It evolves with you as your journey and story is written. Your network grows as you do, so the more you learn and experience life, the more people you will have in your network. It does not happen automatically, but if you commit to networking and want to have meaningful relationships, your network will be abundant.

In a digital world, you have the ability to connect with people from anywhere in the world at almost any time. When you commit to networking, think big and dream big because sometimes the people most willing to help and connect with you are the ones who may intimidate you and/or are the most successful.

Are you committed to networking? Once you make the commitment to begin building and developing your network, move on to step two.

Step 2: Find People You Want to Connect With

You completed the first step to be committed and are ready to network. Now, it is time to start finding the people who you want to network with. The people you will want to connect with are people who have worked in the industries that interest you most. They should be people who have your dream job or appear interesting.

One way to do this is to look up companies and search the about page for people you want to contact. Some companies, depending on their size and structure, will have the contact information listed right there for you. Other companies will only list the names and you will have to find their contact info another way. If this is the case ask your friends or family if they know anyone that works at these companies.

Other ways to find people are to use search engines or social media platforms. LinkedIn is the best social media site for business, but Twitter, Facebook, and Instagram are also good to use for finding information about people as people often place their contact info in their bio.

Kelf Key: Every company uses their own method of email address formatting, so once you have one person's email address you can reach anyone in the company. Do not abuse this and spam everyone in the company, but use this as a tool to strategically reach out to the people who would be best for you to connect with.

Common email formats:

firstnamelastinitial@companyname.com

firstandlastname@companyname.com

firstinitiallastname@companyname.com

Once you have a list of people that you want to connect with and their contact information, move on to step three.

Step 3: Connect With and Set Up an Informational Interview

You now have a list of people who you want to connect with but are not sure about the best way to do it. A lot of people get to this point and then panic because they do not know what to say, when to say it, or how to say it. The three ways that I recommend connecting with people are through referrals, email and LinkedIn.

Now, before we continue, let me explain what an informational interview is. An informational interview is a meeting wherein a job seeker/ networker seeks advice or information from someone in the industry, job, or career field that he/she is interested in. Informational interviews are extremely valuable and are a great way to begin a relationship with people in the roles and fields that you are interested in.

Referrals

Referrals are typically the easiest way to connect with people because it is a *warm* introduction. A warm introduction means that someone you know is offering your name to the person you are interested in connecting with. Once you have the warm introduction, you have a contact and you can ask for a meeting or informational interview. When you ask for the informational interview, tell him/her that you are interested in learning more about what he/she does and if he/she has a few minutes to answer some questions. This can be done in person or however you were referred to the contact. Don't be shy! If you are referred to someone, you already have the "in." More often than not, when you are referred to someone, they will be happy to help and meet with you.

Email

Reaching out through email is one of the most intimate and friendly ways to connect with someone. It shows you have done the research and put in the effort to obtain someone's email. Some of you may think this is creepy, but it really isn't. It shows dedication and ambition and most people will appreciate the hustle. Email is also something that everyone looks at daily, so this is one of the best ways to get the person you are contacting to see your message. The biggest tip when sending an email is to make sure it is personalized and that you emphasize appreciation and gratitude for them taking the time to read your email.

When you initially reach out to connect with someone through email, it is vital that you are respectful of his or her time. You should be very friendly and welcoming as people are very busy and do not want to be bombarded with insincere requests or introductions. This is where you introduce yourself and ask for an informational interview.

LinkedIn

LinkedIn is a terrific resource for reaching out to people for informational interviews, especially in a business setting. According to LinkedIn's about page, LinkedIn is the number one resource for online networking with over 400 million users. Not only can you find almost anyone in business on LinkedIn, but you can learn a thing or two about them before you even reach out by looking at their profile. You can see if you have any similar interests or any connections in common. When you have similar interests or shared connections, it makes it easier to connect.

You have two options to reach out. You can connect with them first and then send a private message or you can send them a message right away via InMail (private messaging on LinkedIn). When sending a connection request, make sure you customize the message and do not use the generic, "I'd like to add you to my professional network on LinkedIn." People who get a lot of connection requests will sometimes decline your request if you don't write a custom message. Remember when you reach out to be polite, gracious, and respectful.

Once you have set up and secured a phone or in-person meeting time with someone, continue to step four.

Step 4: Conducting the Informational Interview

You have successfully reached out and secured some informational interviews with people that you want to learn more about. Typically, informational interviews range from 5-15 minutes depending on the engagement level of conversation and the interviewers schedule.

> *Kelf Key: If you conduct yourself professionally and are genuine, sometimes an informational interview can turn into a job opportunity.*

I know some of you are shy or don't have much experience talking to new people on the phone. Some of you won't have any issue talking with people for fifteen minutes at a time. To make it very easy for anyone's skill level or confidence level, I have broken the informational interview down into three main parts: The Intro, The Convo, and The Goodbye.

The Intro (1-2 minutes)

The Intro is where you make small talk and get comfortable with each other. It is a great place to get a feel for the person you are interviewing.

- Say hello and introduce yourself
- Ask them how their day/week is going
- Thank them for taking the time out of their day to talk with you
- Let them know you are excited to hear more

The Convo (5-10 minutes)

The Convo is the heart of the informational interview. It is the part where you dive in and learn about the person you are interviewing. This is the time to ask any question that you want as long as it is appropriate. You should prepare beforehand to prevent awkward pauses and silences and help make the conversation flow smoothly.

- What was/ is your career path?
- What are your day-to-day responsibilities?
- What is the best part about your job?
- What is your 5 year plan?
- What is the company culture?
- Ask a question specific to their job or industry
- What do you think about the recent partnership between X and Y?
- While working hard to close a deal with Company X, how were you able to effectively manage your other clients?
- Use the flow of the conversation to adapt and ask new questions that relate to the person's answers

Once you are approaching the end of the conversation or the end of your prepared questions, make sure to include something about yourself, even if the interviewer does not ask. A lot of the time people will ask about you and what you want to do. If not, make sure you let them know who you are and your ambitions. This might seem awkward but you do this so they can remember you and so you can share your interests, thus making the interview mutually beneficial. By doing this you engrain yourself into his/her mind so when future opportunities arise, he/she will be more likely to think abut you and consider you more than someone they have never met.

The Goodbye (1-2 minutes)

Having a strong goodbye is crucial because this is where you show your gratitude and further develop the relationship.

- Thank them for their time again
- Offer good luck, congratulations, have a great rest of your day, or something about the conversation that will stick with you after the call
- Let them know that you will be in touch

Step 5: Follow Up and Develop the Relationship

After you finish your informational interview, you need to follow up and say thank you. It can be the same day or day after, but do not wait too long to thank them. When you send them a thank you email, make sure you include:

- Thanking them for taking the time to talk with you
- One thing that you learned
- One takeaway that will stay with you
- That you are excited to continue getting to know each other

FACT: I don't know if you've noticed but giving thanks is a common theme! Show gratitude. People notice and appreciate this!

Kelf Key: Mail a thank you note to their office! It is such a rarity to mail a thank you note in today's world, but it can make all the difference. It's okay to be traditional in this sense. Actually, I recommend it!

Once you have sent your thank you email (and thank you note), check in and update each person you have interviewed every few months. Checking in every so often further develops the relationship and keeps you in their mind, which can lead to recommendations or job referrals down the road. It will also keep you updated on what they are doing and the direction of their career.

Step 6: Enjoy Your Relationships and Mentorships

Stay updated with your connections and don't be afraid to congratulate them on their successes. Even if you are a sophomore in college and they are the VP of Google, everyone loves to be congratulated. Continue to make more connections and use this process to expand your network and enjoy the results. Remember, networking is not just about you. It is about having a mutually beneficial relationship that progresses both of your lives in a positive manner.

The 6 steps to becoming a champion networker:

1. Commit to networking

2. Find people you want to meet and connect with

3. Connect with and set up an informational interview

4. Conduct the informational interview

5. Follow up and develop the relationship

6. Enjoy your new relationships and mentorships

Congratulations! You've successfully completed the networking process and are on your way to becoming a champion networker. Now that you have these relationships, continue to develop them. The better you get to know someone the more beneficial your partnership will be for both you and the person you initially connected with. Feel free to ask for advice or ask if you can help them with anything. Most of the time, the people in your network will be more than willing to help, sometimes even honored that you asked them. Since you are awesome and working hard to improve yourself and meet new people, I've included some example emails, informational interview call scripts, thank you notes, and follow up updates in the Resources for Success section at the end of the book for you to use as templates and references.

Section 2: Leveraging Your Family and Friends for a Job or Contact

Your friends and family are some of your strongest relationships in life, so why not have them help you on your journey to success. The people that love you most are often the most wiling to help; you just have to ask. If you are not close to your family or do not have many friends, ask the people in your life that you do love, respect, and trust. Asking your friends, family, and people that support you for introductions is a great way to build your network because if they are willing to help, you have a very high chance of getting in contact with the person you want to connect with. This is not to say that you are guaranteed a job just because your friends or family know someone in the field you are interested in. What it does mean is that they can provide you with the first introduction and you can take it from there. Sometimes the hardest part is getting the introduction, so this helps expedite the process. The key with asking friends, family and supporters to introduce you to people is to be clear on what you are asking. Many people are afraid of asking even though the answer will be yes a majority of the time. In this situation, do not worry about mixing your personal life with your professional life. All you are doing is asking for an introduction or a recommendation to meet someone, which will give you an advantage.

Many of my friends from college were able to leverage their family and friends to ultimately get a job out of college and this is how they did it.

For purposes of confidentiality, the name of this person has been changed. Uncle Stan secured a job at a Real Estate development company after graduation. He initially met the owner through his dad who set up the introduction. His dad and his current boss are friends, so Uncle Stan asked his dad if his friend would be willing to have a meeting and give Uncle Stan some advice and guidance about real estate. From that conversation Uncle Stan was able to lock up an internship after junior year and now, Uncle Stan works for that company full time. All he did was ask his dad to give his name to his dad's friend so he could learn more. Uncle Stan still had to set up and follow through with the informational interview, send in his resume, and go through the interview process. In the end, Uncle Stan earned his own credibility with this contact and it worked out for him! It all started with him asking his dad to share his name with a professional in Uncle Stan's field of interest.

Ben Badower knew he wanted to work in consulting after growing up around the industry. To find out more about the consulting world, he asked his dad to introduce him to someone at Accenture. Ben's dad worked there prior to his retirement, so Ben leveraged that relationship to meet someone in the industry. He was able to learn a lot about the consulting world and what entry-level jobs entailed. From there, he used this knowledge to apply through USC and because of his great grade point average, extracurricular activities, and solid resume, he was able to get an interview. Ben crushed the interview and now works for Accenture as an analyst.

Max Miller started his college career playing baseball for Monmouth, but transferred to USC after his sophomore year to study communications and be back in his hometown of Los Angeles. He was able to be closer to his family and by being so, he was able to spend more time learning about real estate from his uncle. Real estate became such a huge passion that Max asked his uncle to help him get an internship. After two years of hard work, internships, a knack for talking and a passion for the real estate world, Max got a job with Stone Miller, a very prestigious real estate firm.

These are just a few examples that I decided to share, but there are thousands of these stories. It all starts with having the confidence to ask your friends and family who they know and if they are willing to help. It is very important to understand that getting an introduction or your resume seen does not mean you will get a job. You still have to be qualified and go through the interview process.

Section 3: How Do I Ask My Network for Help Getting a Job?

Building a network is hard enough and now that you have one, you want to make the most of it. You do not want to overstep your relationships, but you also want to get a job or at least get some advice and further your career. This leads us to the million-dollar question. When is it appropriate and how do I ask my network for help with getting a job? One of the most difficult decisions/ questions you will face once you have a network is when is the appropriate time and how to ask your network or people in your network to help you get a job? The answer, it depends. I'm sure you wanted an easy answer, but unfortunately, that is not the case when it comes to this topic. Every person is different which is why building a meaningful relationship is the number one key to networking success. Once you have built that meaningful relationship, it will become more clear as to when and how to ask someone for help with getting a job.

When you feel comfortable with someone in your network, it is okay to ask him/her if he/she knows of any opportunities in his/her company or elsewhere or if he/she knows anyone that would be good to connect with in your desired industry.

Kelf Key: Flip the relationship and pretend you are the one with more experience. If someone asked you for help getting a job, would you feel comfortable and willing to help? If yes, then your relationship is strong enough and you should go for it. If no, continue to build your relationship and become more comfortable in your relationship.

If you only use your network to advance your career, you will never truly reap the benefits of true networking.

Networking is a two way street so when you provide value, your network will as well. Once you realize that networking is all about helping each other out, only then will you be able to maximize your opportunities.

Section 4: 5 Tips for Effective Networking by Jeff Fellenzer

Jeff Fellenzer is a senior lecturer and full time professor at the University of Southern California's Annenberg School of Communication and Journalism, who teaches "Sports, Business, Media" and "Sports and Media Technology." He was chosen one of Annenberg's "most inspiring professors" and in a student survey, his "Sports, Business, Media" class was voted the No. 4 most popular class at USC. A former Los Angeles Times writer/ editor and skilled entrepreneur, he works with students and young professionals around the country on the subjects of networking, resume writing, and interviewing. In this segment, Jeff reveals how he honed his own networking skills and offers tips on how to grow your network and develop great relationships.

"It's all about relationships.

I can't emphasize those words enough. Now more than ever.

At one point early in a long career that has encompassed both sports business and sports media, and now includes helping to develop future generations who will be poised to excel in those fields as a college professor, I realized that every job I had ever held was either a direct or indirect result of tapping into a network I had started building while a student at the University of Southern California.

I met many key sports media members and professional sports team employees through my classes at USC, both when they came to class as guest speakers and when I met them in the field while I was conducting research for class projects (I always picked projects related to my career interests, when given a choice).

If a guest left a business card, while offering to help anyone who asked, I was always the one who called. One prominent Los Angeles sportscaster at the time later told me that of all the students he had spoken to over the years, I was one of two who had actually taken advantage of his offer and followed up with a phone call. The other, by the way, went on to a successful career as a national TV journalist.

So building your network starts early... and never stops.

A few more things to remember about the art of networking:

1. Always have samples of your best work accessible, whether via blogs, podcasts, links to published pieces, etc. Do you have work on YouTube or Twitter that you can send? Is your profile on LinkedIn updated, accurate and streamlined for easy reference?

2. Keep working on your elevator pitch. Practice making a positive impact in front of someone by telling them something about yourself that stands out in a minute or less. Just as if you were suddenly joined in an elevator or bumped into a person who you had always wanted to meet, while waiting for your drink at Starbucks.

   I say this often to students looking for jobs in sports: How do you separate yourself and stand out from the pack? Because everyone does, in some way, stand out and have amazing qualities. That's the first part. The next part is making sure that your uniqueness comes across, whether on your resume or in person. So look at these random close encounters as extraordinary opportunities to let yourself shine!

3. Carefully research your contact person and his/her company. Has his/her job title changed since you first got his/her business card? Are you positive that you know how to spell his/her name correctly? Misspelled names usually result in paper tossed right into the circular files. As the late, great former USC baseball coach, Rod Dedeaux, used to say: *Never make the same mistake once.* Have you found any links to common ground with your new contact person? I always enjoy finding out where a person went to high school. Since I follow high school sports closely, I'm pretty good at knowing prominent sports people from various high schools around the country. It's a fun challenge and a great icebreaker, but there are many others. Find one that works for you.

4. Be patient in an impatient world. You may not hear anything back after an initial email or phone

call but that's okay. Use your best judgment on when to follow up. Handwritten notes are a nice touch. Remember to use a larger type size on your notes because the person reading your correspondence is very likely to be older, and may appreciate not having to strain to read your words.

Sending another note or email two or three weeks later is rarely a problem. In fact, it's often a reminder to your target that he or she forgot to respond to your first note, and many/most times they appreciate that reminder. I always say there's a fine line between being persistent and being a pest. Use your gut feeling. A former student of mine saw a very prominent sports agent at an event once, someone he had met a few years earlier. After debating it for a while, he decided to walk over and say hello to the agent, then laughed while he told the agent about his hesitation. The agent offered a disarming smile and these words of advice for future encounters: 'Always say hello.' I like to put it another way: Students who stay in touch, stay in mind.

5. Do not underestimate the power of just being around. No. 1 on my "Keys to Success in Sports Business" is this one: *Make yourself invaluable.* Someone who has always done that well is a former student of mine. Without having a defined role, this student showed up at the inaugural Front Office Combine in July 2015 in Las Vegas with the intention of just helping out in any way he could, since he knew the organizers. After barely one day of the week-long 'boot camp,' the student had proven himself so invaluable while performing a myriad of vital tasks, typical 'grunt work' that he was hired on the spot. Mission accomplished.

I have been asked this question often over the years: How have you been able to attract high-profile guests to your sports, business, media classes at USC over the years, such as John Wooden, Jerry West, Louie Zamperini, Al Michaels, Bill Walton, Pete Carroll, Jim Nantz, Scott Boras, Jim Lampley, George Raveling, Kevin Love and Casey Wasserman?

Now you know: It's all about relationships!"

As you can see from Jeff's experience and tips, the key to networking is building relationships. Jeff has done it for many years and it has led to some incredible friendships and relationships. Now, he teaches others how to be a successful networker and strives to help the next generation of future stars. As you begin to apply the advice and strategies mentioned in this chapter, focus on being yourself, reaching out to new people, and finding ways to provide value to every person that you meet.

Checklist

- Am I ready to begin networking?
- Did I find people I want to network with?
- Did I reach out to people?
- Have I set up informational interviews?
- Did I follow up and send thank you notes?

Worksheet

Connect with 5 new people on LinkedIn everyday.

Start with people that you know and work on sending custom invitation requests. This will get you in the habit of sending personalized messages, so that when you connect with higher ups and people you don't know, you will be comfortable reaching out. Do this for a month and you will have over 150 connections and a bunch of people to set up informational interviews with.

Find 10 people in your desired field and get their contact info.

It can be anyone from an intern to the CEO. The purpose of this is to familiarize yourself with the process and practice building a list of contacts that you are interested in reaching out to.

Set up 2 informational interviews every week for a month.

Doing this on a consistent basis will help you get in a rhythm and really help you understand and enjoy the conversations. Every call will be different and have a different feel to it, so the more practice the easier it becomes.

Practice asking for advice.

Ask your closest friend for a recommendation on a movie. Even though this might seem menial and unnecessary, it will help build your confidence so you can ask your friends, family, and supporters for something of value later down the road.

Bonus Exercise: For advanced networkers or anyone that thinks they are up for the challenge, practice your networking skills by going up to an attractive person at a bar and ask for his/her number. It doesn't matter if he/she gives you a real or fake number. The point here is to be comfortable asking difficult questions. Maybe, if you're lucky, you'll even get a date out of it.

Chapter 5: Using Social Media and Storytelling to Your Advantage

"Social media is changing the way we communicate and the way we are perceived, both positively and negatively. Every time you post a photo or update your status, you are contributing to your own digital footprint and personal brand."

– Amy Jo Martin

What celebrity is pregnant? What is the score of the game? Who hooked up with who? All of these questions can be answered by almost anyone at any time. Social media is taking over the world and with that so is its presence in your personal and professional life. Social media is a platform that can be used to build your personal brand, communicate with the world and grow your business. It is constantly evolving which is why now more than ever it is important to understand the ins and outs of social media.

Did You Know?

Facebook: 1.59 billion active monthly users as of December 2015[1]

Twitter: 320 million active monthly users[2]

Instagram: 400 million active monthly users[3]

LinkedIn: 400 million active monthly users[4]

Snapchat: 100 million active monthly users[5]

YouTube: 1+ billion users[6]

Pinterest: 100 million active monthly users[7]

---

[1] http://newsroom.fb.com/company-info/
[2] https://about.twitter.com/company
[3] https://www.instagram.com/press/?hl=en
[4] https://press.linkedin.com/about-linkedin
[5] https://www.snapchat.com/ads
[6] https://www.youtube.com/yt/press/statistics.html
[7] http://venturebeat.com/2015/09/16/pinterest-finally-shares-its-size-100m-monthly-active-users-and-counting/

Section 1: Sharing a Positive Message

Your social media presence is what I like to call your online personality. The way you interact with people online is directly related to the way you interact with people in person. Just as in person, if you are mean, unfriendly, or insincere people will not want to connect with you. If you are friendly, considerate, honest, or a joy to be around, people will want to connect with you. Your social media presence is a way for you to express yourself and share content with the world instantaneously. As the world continues to become more digital, it is vital that you practice good habits on social media.

The reason why it is so important to create a social media presence that reflects your personality is because we live in a time of extreme judgment. As soon as you press send/publish/post, your content is released to the world and people start looking at it. They start formulating opinions of your content and will judge your character off of what you post on social media. I'm not saying that it is right to judge someone or his or her character for what they post, but that's the way it is. That is why it is so important to focus on having your online personality be in sync with your in person personality.

Think about when people you follow post about their family or a new job. They are often smiling and people want to engage with them. You are excited for them and give them a like or a comment. When people post about getting drunk over the weekend or doing drugs, it does not reflect well on them, and successful people will most likely try to stay away from these posts and/or the individuals who are posting such information. I believe that we all have our unique personalities and we should be proud of them, but it is important to remember that what people see on social media does not tell the whole story. Make sure to post what you are comfortable with everyone seeing at any time.

Section 2: Social Media in the Hiring Process

"Once you put it out there, even if you think it is private, it's out there for good, so only post what you want everyone to see."

– Sheri Omens Kelfer, Adjunct Professor at the University of Southern California

Social media is becoming an instrumental part of the hiring process. Recruiters are checking social media as a preliminary measure to quickly eliminate applicants.

According to the Huffington Post[8], over 52% percent of employers are using social sites to screen job candidates during the hiring process. These social network checks have become almost as common as reference checks and criminal background checks.

This number is only going to continue to increase, so it would be wise to make sure your online personality is professional, consistent, and reflects your true personality.

I know what most of you are saying to yourself right now. "I have my social media set to private, so I don't need to listen to this schmuck tell me what to do." Well, even if you set your settings to private, recruiters can find ways to access your information and see what you are posting. You would be surprised as to how much information that you think is private is actually available to the public. Recruiters will go so far as to add you on social networking sites and then search your photos and posts dating all the way back to your very first one.

The reason recruiters and companies look at your social media is to see if you are really the same person as you say you are on your resume or in your interview. They want to be sure that when they hire you, there will not be any

---

[8] http://www.huffingtonpost.com/genia-stevens-mba/how-employers-use-social-_b_8914526.html

added surprises. They want to make sure that you are not going to reflect their company poorly or do something that would jeopardize their reputation.

I'll give you a great example at the lengths recruiters will go to find out who you are. During the final months before the NFL Draft, Brock Vereen was interviewing with teams as part of the draft process. One of the teams gave him a piece of paper that included a tweet he posted from his sophomore year in college and asked him to explain it. Luckily for him it wasn't bad, but this just goes to show you how important it is to only post what you want the world to see.

Another reason they look at your social media is to see what you are tweeting about or posting about. Recruiters like to see that you are posting about the industry you are trying to break into because it shows that you are knowledgeable and committed. Let's say you are applying for a job in sports or entertainment. When a recruiter looks at your Twitter, you want to make sure that your feed is full of tweets and engagement with others in that field. Recruiters want to see that what you do for fun is related to the industry you are applying to. It makes recruiters feel more confident that you are a serious candidate.

While it might seem unfair that recruiters are adding you on social media or searching through your online presence to find out about you, it is a smart move. Recruiters are trying to find the best talent for their company and they want to make sure they hire great people. At any moment, content can go viral so they are trying to maximize the reward and minimize the risks by doing this. If you don't like the fact that recruiters will research you, then don't post anything you wouldn't want people seeing.

Section 3: 5 Characteristics of a Killer Social Media Presence

These characteristics will be a way for you to not only pass a recruiter's test, but also give you an advantage and help build your personal brand.

Post Photos of Your Friends and Family Having Fun

People always love to see photos of people with their parents, cousins, best friends, or anyone that has a positive impact on you. It brings people joy when you post about the ones you care about. Whether you are cooking a killer recipe for avocado fries or playing football at the park, people enjoy seeing others having fun with the people they care about.

Show the World What You Are Up to Professionally

Share with the world what you do professionally. Not only is it a great way to spark a conversation with someone about what you do, but it is also a chance to make a new contact that could lead to new business. Also, posting about what you do professionally will tell a lot about your character. I know some of you love to post photos in your suits or dresses, so keep that up because looking classy is always a good thing.

Share Your Experiences of Community Involvement

If you are involved in extracurricular activities or take part in community service, share that with the world. It is a great way to inform everyone about the cause you are supporting. This builds an emotional connection with your audience. It is also a great way for people to see your compassion and willingness to help others.

Post Photos of Your Travels

Besides being some of the most amazing photos online, posting photos of your travels goes a long way. People love to stay updated on where you are in the world. Even more so, they love seeing what you do when you are travelling. What food are you eating? What activities are you participating in? What museum did you visit? What club did you go to? Posting photos of your travels can also tell a story about you and your willingness to try new things or your openness to new surroundings.

Share Your Interests With Your Audience

People love to see what your interests are and the activities that you participate in. It can be inspirational quotes, food, dogs, fashion or anything that you enjoy doing. When you share your interests with your audience, it can generate like-minded people reaching out to you and new opportunities.

> *Kelf Key: Lewis Howes is incredible at this. He is always posting motivational quotes and sharing photos of his podcast guests. He is constantly engaging with his audience and giving them a glimpse into his personal life. If you haven't heard of him, you should definitely check him out at LewisHowes.com.*

Section 4: Superstar Social Media Users

Larry Fitzgerald @LarryFitzgerald · 11 Sep 2015
Remembering the tragedy & heroism that occurred on 9/11. My gratitude to all who serve to keep us safe #NeverForget

NEVER FORGET.
09.11.2001

↩   ↻ 565   ♥ 616   •••

Here is a tweet from Larry Fitzgerald who is one of the most respected football players of all time. Larry uses his account to positively promote himself and the things he is passionate about.

Beyonce is Queen. It is as simple as that. Her social media presence is filled with amazing pictures that share her talents and unbelievable character with the world.

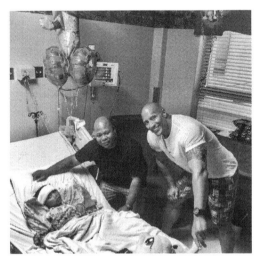

therock

653k likes   3d

therock Joi wasn't feeling very well when I surprised her at the Pediatric Specialty Ward. Managed to get a slight smile out of her 😊 and had a good chat with her father. Hope you guys get to go back home to New Jersey very soon. Stay strong honey ~ DJ

Log in to like or comment.

The Rock is a legend. He always shares posts thanking his fans, showing what project he is working on, and he posts about his workouts to keep his audience wanting more.

These three examples, although they are celebrities, do an incredible job promoting themselves and sharing a positive message with their audience.

Larry, Beyonce, or The Rock: If you see this, I would love to meet you.

Checklist

- Does my social media presence reflect my personality?
- Am I thinking about the message I am sending each time I post a picture, tweet, or update?
- Am I posting about and engaging with the industry I want to break into?

Worksheet

- What are 3 words that describe your current social media presence?
- What are 3 words you want people to think of when they see your social media?
- Compare the two lists and see if they match. If they do, great job! If not, then either delete old posts or start posting new posts that will transform the way your audience sees you.

Chapter 6: Putting it All Together

Throughout this book, you have learned how to find a career that you are passionate about, create an irresistible resume, crush every interview, build an extensive network and tell a story through social media. To put it all together, I want to share some stories of people who have used the strategies and techniques in this book to help show you that this stuff really works. This information will help you in so many ways, ultimately resulting in the next part of your career journey.

Brandon Berman is a senior at the University of Southern California with a bright future in entertainment ahead of him. Brandon is an extremely talented networker and it stems from two things: his desire to make meaningful relationships and his confidence. At the time of this book, he has worked for NBCUniversal, Sony Pictures, Amazon Studios, Snapchat, Creative Artists Agency, and Showtime Networks, all while taking a full course load. He interned at all of these amazing companies because he became friends with all of his professors, utilized his fraternity and asked his family for help. He was not afraid of failure or rejection and because of that he was able to develop some incredible relationships. He then used those relationships to find a connection to each of the internships and once he had that, he was in.

Easton Fier is the Director of Brand for Rufus Labs and has been able to work his way up from intern to head of marketing for the company in just one year out of college. I don't know about you, but I think that's pretty incredible. Besides hard work and having a knack for marketing, Easton is proud of who he is. During his initial interview for his internship, he used his energetic and lively personality to bring his resume to life. He prepared whole-heartedly, learned about trends in the wearable technology world, and had questions ready to be answered at the end of his interview. His professionalism, preparedness and personality were the three Ps that got him his start at Rufus Labs.

Blake Pinsker is the Marketing Director for MVMT Watches, but he did not start there. He ended college and took a job with a real estate company just so he could pay the bills and say he had a job. He knew that wasn't what he wanted to do for the rest of his life so he continued to expand his network and look for jobs that interested him. At the same time he asked his friend who is a successful entrepreneur for some advice regarding a crowdfunding campaign. He stayed in contact with his friend and less than a year later his friend hired him to work in marketing for MVMT Watches. Had he not continued to develop his relationship and ask for advice, his friend might never have known that Blake was interested in marketing. He never asked for a job, but because Blake was genuine and interested in learning, he stood out to his friend as a great candidate and eventually became the newest member of the MVMT Watches Family.

Taylor Harrison is a Paralegal for Universal Music Group. As a student athlete at Cornell, Taylor was constantly busy and didn't have much time to work while in school. Instead of letting her lack of work experience prevent her from succeeding, she told her story through a beautifully formatted and content driven resume. She was a student with great grades, a collegiate athlete, had two minors, and was in a sorority. To add even more personality to her resume, she included that she took a Rock music class because she loved music. The story she told on her resume gave her the edge over the competition and landed her the current job.

Rahul Bansal is a Production Assistant at Anonymous Content. He has always focused on making his interviews less quizzical and more personal. His resume is great and he is always going out for drinks to network, but one of the biggest reasons Rahul has been so successful in getting internships and jobs is because of his approach to interviews. Once he gets an interview, he spends time researching and learning everything he can so when he arrives, he will have plenty to talk about. Instead of allowing his interviews to be a Q & A, Rahul makes his interviews as conversational as possible. His best interviews end with him and the interviewer talking about things that aren't even entertainment related. During his last interview before getting his job at Anonymous Content, he ended up talking to the interviewer about pickup basketball and sports related injuries. The emotional connection that Rahul built with the interviewer made Rahul stand out and get the job.

Chase Lehner is an Assistant to Simon Halls at Slate PR. One thing that Chase did was stay true to himself from the moment he became interested in entertainment and PR. He used his internships to develop relationships with the higher ups because he knew that in order to make his internship a full time job he would need to stand out. Because of his willingness to go above and beyond and connect with the higher ups, he was eventually referred to his current job. Once he was in the door at Slate PR, he used his charm and charismatic personality to nail the interview.

Emily Dods is an Assistant Integrated Media Strategist at Wieden + Kennedy which is one of the best advertising agencies in the country. Before getting this job, Emily didn't know exactly what job she wanted so she looked at her interests and tried to find jobs and companies that were a great fit with her personality. She narrowed down her job search to a top tier advertising agency in New York or San Francisco and began to network and meet people so she could learn more and figure out how to get her foot in the door. After networking with a bunch of people in advertising, Emily met with someone from Wieden + Kennedy at an info session. The guy loved her energy and asked for her resume. The next day she was brought in for an interview. In Emily's case, it all started by figuring out what she wanted to do, networking with people in her desired position, developing a relationship, having a strong resume and then having a memorable and impressive interview.

Chase LaVine is a Client Relationship Specialist in Vanguard's Flagship division. Chase knew he wanted to be in the finance world and was willing to move wherever to get his career started. When Vanguard appeared at San Diego State, Chase's alma mater, he met with the recruiter and gave him his resume. There were a bunch of people who did this but because of Chase's well-formatted and diverse resume, he was able to move on to the interview stage. Since Vanguard interviews a lot of people for their entry level positions, Chase had to figure out a way to stand out during his interview. He did this by researching everything he possibly could about the interviewers, the company, the financial industry and by the time his interview came, he was prepared and felt confident. The effort paid off and after a flawless interview Chase got the job.

Sasha Spivak is a Stanford graduate working in the technology industry while running a successfully funded Kickstarter business called Boxly. As a freshman at the prestigious Stanford University, Sasha knew she would have to find ways to stand out from all of the other brilliant and amazing people. She spent the majority of her underclassmen years looking at her interests and figuring out what she really enjoyed. She even went to Japan and lived with a host family who didn't speak any English in order to figure out what brings her the most happiness. While she was in Japan, she was able to get a job by being honest and upfront with the company. Her skill set wasn't exactly what they were looking for, but in a culture based on respect, willingness to learn, and honesty, Sasha's desire for growth landed her the job. This led to her returning to Stanford for her final two years where she spent her junior year focusing on classes that were engaging and passion filled. She spent her senior year applying for as many jobs as she could. She spent hours combing the Alumni Network looking for people to contact. She even upgraded her LinkedIn membership so she could reach out to more people. By the end of her senior year, she had over 50 interviews and multiple job offers. Sasha's story is an example of how hard work, finding out who you are, discovering your passion, and connecting with desirable people leads to happiness and success.

The last story I want to share was told to me by Jeff Fellenzer, senior lecturer at the University of Southern California:

"One of the students in my spring 2016 "Sports, Business, Media" class at USC had reached out to me a few times through the first couple months of the semester, interested in sharing his career goals with me, which started with becoming general manager of the Los Angeles Dodgers. I could relate to that one, since that had also been one of my early dreams years ago. One night after class, he was peppering me with questions and comments, and clearly was in no hurry to leave, in spite of it being close to 10 p.m. He seemed mildly frustrated that everything wasn't moving faster for him, that he hadn't been able to land an internship yet in sports even though he was only a sophomore. Finally, an idea hit me and I suggested that he contact my friend and one-time USC teaching partner, former Dodgers general manager Fred Claire, now a partner in a baseball analytics company. Fred still kept regular hours at his office in Pasadena, and always welcomed my students who wanted to learn more about baseball and sports business. I could see the excitement in his face, and heard it in his voice. He knew all about Fred Claire.

Sure enough, he set up an appointment with Fred, who quickly learned of the student's interest in baseball analytics when they met. Fred needed someone to attend the prestigious MIT Sloan Sports Analytics Conference, coming up in a couple of weeks in Boston, to do some research and represent his company. My student was invited to join Fred's team, and fly to Boston with another student intern. Fred emailed me as the conference was about to begin, amazed at the chain of events that had just taken place: the student speaks to me, I contact Fred, the student meets Fred, he's offered an internship, and then ends up being sent on a paid visit to the Sloan conference, a dream-come-true for this young man.

Right place, right time? Sure, but it happened because this student had taken the initiative and was persistent with me, then took my suggestions and ran with them. Soon after he was on a plane headed to Boston."

After reading these stories, it is apparent that all of these strategies work together to achieve success. Some people use different methods to stand out whether it is their network, resume, or interviewing skills, but overall, everyone puts these elements together to make themselves stand out and gain an advantage over their competition.

Final Words from Kelf

Congratulations! You did it. You found time to read a book whether you are in high school, college, or beyond. I know it must have been hard, but I hope you have learned at least a few things. I know I have provided you with a lot of tips and strategies to think about and use to your advantage, but now you have the information and knowledge to achieve your dreams and elevate yourself to the next level of your life. Here are a few thoughts I'd like to share with you before you start celebrating your accomplishments as you get started applying all of this great information.

How Much You Succeed is Up to You

You determine the outcome of your life. Don't let others tell you what you can or cannot do. If you want to be better than all of the other candidates in the job market you can. You just have to believe in yourself and put in the work. If you have a hard time believing in yourself, there is no shame in seeking help.

This is a Process

Figuring out what you want to do with your life, resume building, interviewing, and networking are all part of the journey. Each of these steps takes time and will require hard work and dedication. The best investment you can make in life is in yourself, so pay your dues, enjoy the process, and embrace the success.

Be Proud of Yourself

You are your own person and you offer something that no one else can. No matter where your journey takes you, it is important to stay true to yourself and take pride in being different. If we were all the same, there would be no struggle and there would be no enjoyment of success when you overcome that struggle.

You Are Not Alone

No matter what your background is or where you come from, we are all in this together. Everyone has to start somewhere so whether you are searching for your first internship or 3rd job, lean on the people that matter most to you to help you get where you want to be and do not forget to be there for them, too.

Have Fun!

I can't say this enough but have fun. Celebrate the little victories because when you make it to the top, you will want to remember where you started from and see all that you have been able to achieve.

The Fundamental Mindset

As you go through this process, I want you to think about these three principles. For every new opportunity, use these as guidance and you will always be able to enjoy whatever life brings.

- Develop Your Mindset
- Define Your Success
- Discover Your Journey

THANK YOU SO MUCH!

I am so happy to share my first book with all of you. It really means the world to me that you purchased this book in order better yourself.

Resources for Success

Sample Informational Interview

Me: Hello Sarah! Thanks so much for making some time to chat with me today. How was your weekend?

Sarah: Hi Jake! Thanks for reaching out to me. My weekend was great! What can I help you with?

Me: I was hoping to learn a little more about you and your role with the company. I have a few questions that I'd like to ask you if that is okay?

Sarah: Sure thing. Ask away.

Me: To begin, what has been your career path and journey up till this point?

Sarah: XXXXX

Me: That's awesome. Seems like you have had a lot of fun on your way to your current role. What are some of your day-to-day responsibilities?

Sarah: XXXXX

Me: That's very interesting. I never knew that. What would you say is your favorite part of your job?

Sarah: XXXXX

Me: It appears you really like what you do. Do you see yourself staying in this role in 5 years or where do you think you will be in your career?

Sarah: XXXXX

Me: My last question is do you have any advice for someone trying to break into the industry?

Sarah: XXXXX. Can you tell me a little more about yourself and what you want to do?

Me: Absolutely. I am currently a junior at USC majoring in Business Administration and minoring in Sports Media Studies. My goal is to work in sports, specifically on the marketing side.

Sarah: Well Jake, it seems like you are well on your way. If there is ever anything I can do to help, please let me know.

Me: Thanks Sarah! I really enjoyed getting to know more about you and your job. Have a great rest of your week and I look forward to staying in touch!

Sample Thank You Note for Informational Interview

Hello (name of person you interviewed),

Thank you so much for taking the time to talk with me yesterday. I really enjoyed learning about your career path and journey. I think that what you do for (company name) is truly making a difference in the world. I will definitely try to always incorporate helping others in whatever I do in life. Thank you again and I look forward to furthering our relationship.

Best,
Your Name

Sample Thank You Note for On-Site Interview

Hello (name of interviewer),

Thank you for taking the time to interview me. I learned a lot about the company and your role with them. Your energy and passion for your job confirmed my desire to be apart of the team. Thanks again and I am looking forward to hearing your decision.

Best,
Your Name

Sample Follow Up Email about Decision After Interview

Hello (name of interviewer),

How was your weekend? I wanted to follow up about my interview. You mentioned that you would let me know your decision about a week after. It's been two weeks since my interview so I wanted to check in and see if you had made a decision or if I am still in consideration for the job? I am still very excited to potentially have the chance to work with you and everyone else at (company name). Have a great rest of your day and I will talk to you soon.

Thanks,
Your Name

Sample Follow Up/ Update Email About New Job

Hello (name of contact),

How are you doing? I hope everything has been going well over at (name of company they work for). I wanted to update you and let you know that I received an internship with (company name). I used some tips that you gave me the last time we spoke and it definitely helped. Anyways, I hope all is well and if there is ever anything you need me to do, please let me know. I'd be happy to help. Talk to you soon!

Best,
Your Name

Sample Email Update About Your Life/ Building the Relationship

Hello (name of contact),

I hope you had a great weekend and your week is off to a great start. I wanted to let you know that I am still pursuing my passion of being in the (name of industry). I am hoping to finish school next semester and I can't wait to get started in the real world. I always think about your advice about being open minded and it has helped me in many situations. I hope everything is going well for you and I look forward to connecting soon.

Best,
Your Name

Sample Email for Cold Networking Opportunity

Hello (name of person),

How are you? My name is Max Jackson and I am a senior at the University of Southern California majoring in business administration and minoring in advertising. I am very interested in (company name) and learning more about the company. I would love to set up a time to discuss more about what you do. Please let me know if you have any available time even if it is just a few minutes. Thank you for your time and I look forward to speaking with you!

Thanks,
Your Name

Sample Email for Personalized LinkedIn Connection Request

Hello (name of person),

I recently came across your profile and I am interested in what you are up to. I would love to connect and learn more about you and your job.

- Your Name

Sample Email for LinkedIn Networking Message Once Connected

Hi (name of person),

Thank you for connecting with me! To tell you a little more about myself, I am a sophomore at the University of Florida majoring in accounting. I am extremely interested in learning more about the accounting world and how I can combine my accounting education with my passion for entertainment. I noticed that you were able to do that with you current job and I would love to hear how that came to be. Would you be interested in setting up a time to speak with me? Even if it is just a few minutes, I would be happy to schedule a time. Thank you and I look forward to connecting.

Thanks,
Your Name

Sample Email for Connecting with a Mutual Colleague

Hello (name of person),

I saw on LinkedIn that we are both connected to (name of mutual connection). She is a great friend of mine and is doing amazing things for the (company name). I was wondering if you would be available to set up a time to connect as I would love to learn more about your career path. Looking forward to hearing how you are connected to (name of mutual connection) and talking to you soon!

Thanks,
Your Name

Sample Email for Asking a Friend or Family Member for Help With an Introduction

Hello (name of family or friend),

How are you? It was great seeing you at Emily's birthday gathering last weekend. It's been too long, but I enjoyed catching up and learning about what you have been up to. I wanted to follow up with you about the person you thought would be good for me to meet and talk to. Would you mind sending me their contact information? Thanks again for doing this and I will be sure to let you know how it goes. Have a great rest of your week and I hope to see you again soon.

Thanks,
Your Name

Sample Email for Students Talking to Students

Hello (name of friend),

What's up? That party on Saturday was pretty awesome. It was such a great surprise to see you there. I know you mentioned that your parents or friend might be good for me to talk to about my future, so I was wondering if you could put me in touch with them? I can text, email, or call; whatever is easiest for them. Thanks in advance and I will see you around.

Best,
Your Name

Notes

1. http://newsroom.fb.com/company-info/

2. https://about.twitter.com/company

3. https://www.instagram.com/press/?hl=en

4. https://press.linkedin.com/about-linkedin

5. https://www.snapchat.com/ads

6. https://www.youtube.com/yt/press/statistics.html

7. http://venturebeat.com/2015/09/16/pinterest-finally-shares-its-size-100m-monthly-active-users-and-counting/

8. http://www.huffingtonpost.com/genia-stevens-mba/how-employers-use-social-_b_8914526.html

Made in the USA
Lexington, KY
09 May 2018